5 Rules for White Belts

By Chris Matakas

Contents

The Impetus for This Book

I opened my own Jiu Jitsu academy in September 2017. Without the experience to properly navigate holidays, we operated with regular hours on Halloween night. There were no kids in either of the youth classes and our first adult class had just a handful of students. With that class coming to a close, and no one awaiting the next, it looked as though I might be having an early night.

Minutes before the second class was to start, in walked Stefan, one of our newest white belts. What was to be an early night proved more beneficial than any reading or writing I would have done with that time.

Stefan and I took the hour to check in with his progress. Having only taken four classes, nearly all of Jiu Jitsu was unknown territory for him. He had learned a few techniques but had not yet received a conceptual framework through which to understand these techniques, the principles they embody, and their proper application.

I asked Stefan very purposeful, vague questions to try to understand the current lens through which he viewed Jiu Jitsu. He is an articulate man capable of voicing his own ignorance, a rare gift we should all seek to cultivate, and he was able to properly convey the confusion he was experiencing in training.

We used his specific questions about techniques to articulate the principles, themes, and lessons they embody. I may have had even more fun than Stefan, as I was excited with the challenge presented to me:

I had one hour with which to help a new student construct a conceptual framework through which to interpret his training.

By the end of the class, Stefan's eyes illuminated with a sense of possibility. Through a discussion, and the purposeful practice of a few techniques, he came to understand that Jiu Jitsu is far more accessible than he had thought. Though its vastness rivals our limitation, Jiu Jitsu could be codified into a handful of positions, principles, and concepts. He came to the school that night not knowing what Jiu Jitsu was and left with a heading for his compass and the course plotted ahead.

It was a productive night. Stefan had grown tremendously as a student. I think I grew even more as a teacher. We were now closer as friends, and we both left more excited about our roles within the academy than when we arrived that evening.

That night I went home thinking, *Man, I wish I could have that kind of quality time with all our new students.* But the limited hours in the day won't allow it. So I went to the whiteboard, and just hours after my time with Stefan, began outlining this book.

I have written much about Jiu Jitsu these past ten years. Most of this writing has focused on using Jiu Jitsu as a tool for personal development, with a small percentage being concerned with the actual technical development of the practitioner. Of that, most has been geared toward the advanced student, focusing primarily on principles whose practice requires an extensive understanding of techniques and their relationships to each other.

I have written very little to the uninitiated, the aspiring student who has just begun his or her journey. This brief book is that attempt.

I hope to give the beginning white belt a conceptual framework through which to interpret Jiu Jitsu, to make his or her education accessible and growth certain. And we must not under-estimate the value of this pursuit. Our technical development in this art often parallels the progress of our humanity. We seek to master this craft so that we master ourselves along the way.

To the best of my current knowledge, this is everything you need to know during your initiation phase, to better understand this wonderful journey on which you are about to embark.

Let's begin.

Toward What Shall We Aim

Before we discuss the five rules for white belts, we must first understand what these rules are attempting to elicit; we need to have a clearly defined goal. We rarely achieve anything noteworthy without purposefully seeking that thing. If we do not know toward what we move, we won't get there; there are too many variables to shift us off the course we have not properly defined.

The aim is mastery.

When we watch skilled black belts train, their movements seem effortless. They are always in a safe position from which to attack, and they string those attacks together as though all of Jiu Jitsu was one movement. The experienced practitioner breathes calmly with a serene face, and with the least amount of effort always seems to arrive at his or her predetermined goal.

But how do we define mastery? What is this elusive skill the masters embody which we all seek to emulate?

We can define mastery as efficacy; a blend of efficiency and effectiveness. The master is able to utilize a minimum effective dose, moving just enough to be maximally effective while minimizing the effort required to be so. This definition reveals a fundamental truth:

Mastery is not a final point at which to arrive; it is a continuum of infinite degrees upon which we move.

Our goal is to continually move along this continuum, away from aimless exertion and toward purposeful and effective movement performed in a way which maximizes efficacy while minimizing exertion.

This is the goal toward which we aim, and our job as beginning practitioners is to learn to use this metric to gauge the worthwhileness of our actions. To better understand this principle, we will rely on the games of our youth.

The Mortal Kombat Principle

Most of us played video games growing up. A staple in my adolescence was Mortal Kombat, a fighting game in which two players battle one another, using various kinds of attacks unique to the character the player chooses, in an attempt to completely diminish your partner's health meter, as he seeks to do the same to you. Whoever runs out of health first, loses.

This serves as a great analogy for the training of Jiu Jitsu.

We and our training partners possess a finite amount of energy. Our goal when training is to use this energy in the most efficient way, retaining as much of ours as possible while forcing our training partners to use excessive amounts of theirs.

Should we succeed in this endeavor, we deplete our partner's reserves and force them into disadvantageous positions from which we capitalize.

This creates two simple and correlated guidelines for action:

1) Seek to maintain as much of your energy as possible.
2) Create opportunities in which your partner consumes his or her energy inefficiently.

To the degree that we do this, our partner's health meter will go down at a rate faster than ours, and we will greatly increase our probability of achieving success (positional advancement or submission) during the training session. We must seek to achieve this lopsided energy expenditure to the furthest extent we are capable.

Now, let's understand how to do it.

How Does One Operate Efficiently?

Our shared goal is to make Jiu Jitsu as accessible as possible. We must clearly articulate the goal, and the many sub-goals which comprise it, if we are to achieve our intended result.

Efficiency in Jiu Jitsu can be understood through four aspects:

1. How to move
2. From where to move
3. With what to move (to be discussed in Rule #2)
4. Why to move (to be discussed in Rule #2)

One by one, we will study these fundamental aspects of Jiu Jitsu to better understand our goal.

How to move: The Playful Sphere

Our language reveals our world. Our vocabulary and the etymology of our words have much to teach us. Especially in Jiu Jitsu, the common phrases we use reveal how to optimally practice the art.

1) "Play"

Those who wrestle are called wrestlers. Those who practice Judo, Judokas,

Jiu Jitsu practitioners refer to themselves as "players," and this reveals an important truth:

We are meant to play Jiu Jitsu. It is a beautiful game of physical, mental, and spiritual exertion, in which we seek to manifest our will, bending our training partner's will (and body) to ours, to advance position and achieve submission, while negating his or her attempts to do the same.

You do not work games; you work at the office. You play games.

Jiu Jitsu is meant to be played. When we are training Jiu Jitsu, we are not fighting. Our training partners are not our opponents. They are not an obstacle to be overcome with great force and effort. Our training partners are fellow players with whom we work together to play Jiu Jitsu on the way to becoming better versions of ourselves.

Our teammates are not our competition; they are the greatest tools in our development.

2) "Rolling"

We defined mastery as a movement toward efficiency. This efficiency is most clearly demonstrated in our movements. We call live training "rolling" for a reason; we are to flow smoothly as we transition between positions.

When beginning students start live training, they resemble a cube rather than a sphere. They topple violently from position to position, like a cube falling on its side, with sudden starts and stops that are aggressive and inefficient.

The experienced player rolls like a sphere. The master glides from position to position, with no clear distinction between them. This is the goal toward which we aim. Moving like a sphere ensures we minimize expenditure of our finite energy.

The goal is to move like a playful sphere. Now that we know how to move, we must understand from where are we to move.

From Where to Move: Functionally Strong Postures

In most of your training, you will be either carrying a load or moving against resistance. To do so efficiently, we must maintain positions of functionally strong postures.

A functionally strong posture is one in which we carry loads in the most ergonomic way, with maximal recruitment of major muscle groups combined with skeletal positioning which most optimally bears resistance.

Said in another way, we want to minimize our rate of perceived exertion.

Our health meter will maintain to the degree that we can lighten the load we carry and lessen the resistance against which we move. This is achieved by maintaining functionally strong posture and putting our partner in functionally weak postures.

1) Functional Strong Postures: Right Angles

Physics are physics, and its laws apply whether building houses in the world or positions in Jiu Jitsu. Architects build with right angles for a reason: this is a means to efficiently carry a structural load.

We do the same in Jiu Jitsu, but rather than building with wood and concrete, we build with our limbs and spine. When framing (using our arms to create space), we want to carry the load in the most efficient way by creating right angles.

Whether using frames when on bottom, in side control, or posturing on top, inside the closed guard, (when our spine is almost perpendicular to the ground, resembling a right angle), creating these structurally strong angles allows us to carry a load and meet resistance in the most optimal way while minimizing energy expenditure.

2) Functionally Weak Postures

The beauty of Jiu Jitsu is that all lessons are binary: when we learn what we want to achieve, we learn what to deny our training partners.

Maintaining functionally strong postures minimizes our energy expenditure. Forcing our partners into functionally weak postures maximizes their energy expenditure.

Whenever possible, and it is always possible, we seek to put our partners into inefficient positions. This can be done myriad ways:

- Disalign their spine.
- Force them to carry weight with sub-optimal frames (often less than or more than 90 degrees, in a non-linear fashion)
- Off balance them to manipulate their center of mass

Without getting too technical, as you will intuitively learn how to do this through training, simply focus on making your partners work harder for what they want. You will achieve this by forcing them to move and carry loads inefficiently from functionally weak postures. Having done so, you will drain your partner's finite energy at a much faster rate, leaving them less capable of advancing position or achieving a submission.

This continued pursuit of efficiency leads us to the consummate Jiu Jitsu metaphor, killing the monster when it's small.

Kill The Monster When It's Small

The most efficient way to deal with a problem is to not allow the problem to manifest itself in the first place. As Ben Franklin said,

"An ounce of prevention is worth a pound of cure."

The immediacy with which we confront a problem matches the effort required to do so. I have always found the following metaphor useful:

Imagine you live in a mythical world. You stumble across a dragon's egg in the woods outside your village. You have two options: 1) leave it be, or 2) squash the egg.

That egg has the potential to become a dragon, and therefore, in a sense, is a dragon: an adversary which can only be combated with massive resources of time, energy, and health. The pragmatic response is to squash the dragon while it is an egg.

These "eggs" present themselves in every moment of training.

While playing guard, our training partner makes a grip on our pants which leads to a guard pass, which turns into us being mounted, then turning our back to escape and getting choked. We must learn to defend that pant grip (the egg) with the sincerity with which we defend a choke (the dragon), because that pant grip is the choke in its early stages of development.

The embodiment of this conceptual framework distinguishes the novice from the master. You will see considerable improvement in your training when you begin to view the minutiae of Jiu Jitsu through this lens.

Summary

Mastery lies on an infinite continuum, one on which we daily strive to advance. This advancement comes in the way of efficacy, becoming effective by becoming efficient.

This efficiency is quantified by your rate of perceived exertion, the sense of how hard you are working. Your effectiveness is measured by your ability to advance position and attain submissions, while preventing your partner from doing the same.

This is practiced by attending to the "Mortal Kombat Principle," as you playfully move like a sphere, "killing" the monsters in their adolescence. This is what the beginning student, to the best of my understanding, should focus on.

Now we turn to the five rules which, should you embody them, will lead to your acquiring great skill in this discipline as you strive toward your highest self.

Rule #1- Remember That You Are A Work In Progress

The greatest initial obstacle to skill development is often one's mindset. Many of us inherit expectations and beliefs from our culture. Our society does not praise failure, it tacitly devalues or overtly chastises those who miss the mark.

Our relationship to failure is a predictor of the joy and effectiveness of our practice. Skill acquisition is cyclical: we must fail, digest that failure and assimilate its lessons into new modes of behavior, and then act again with improved probability of success. We make constant iterations until we achieve our intended result.

Having done so, we simply begin again in a new endeavor. Past success is the antecedent to future failure. To improve we must not rest on our laurels, we cast them aside and immediately seek a new challenge.

Though the challenges come in many forms, they are of the same nature:

We play at the edge of our current abilities, the precipice of the unknown beyond explored territory (and our associated stress-tested efficacy) where unfamiliar variables force our continued evolution. Whether we are a white belt or a black belt, the process is the same; the color of your belt cannot save you from the necessity of failure.

Nor deem the irrevocable Past
As wholly wasted, wholly vain,
If, rising on its wrecks, at last
To something nobler we attain.
-Henry Wadsworth Longfellow

It is irrevocable; it is necessary. And it is the only way of nobility. The bulk of your time at white belt will be spent in failure. We must learn to see these failings as the prerequisite for success; this is us as an egg on our way to becoming a dragon.

"Rather than be someone with no flaws, be the entity that continually realizes its flaws and overcomes them."- Jordan Peterson

This is the perspective we must embody. Rather than trying not to fail in training, we should seek out purposeful failure in the most productive way, confronting our incompetence in perpetuity.

The best black belts in the world feel as though they have barely glimpsed Jiu Jitsu. The more skill we develop, the more skill there is to be developed.

"We live on an island surrounded by a sea of ignorance. As our island of knowledge grows, so does the shore of our ignorance."- John Archibald Wheeler

Not only must we learn to embrace failure, we must see it as a metric for progress. Failure is synonymous with growth. We must continually realize and rectify our flaws, so that we may find more flaws.

This process is infinite.

Understanding the Unknown: The Hero's Journey

Joseph Campbell taught mythology at Sarah Lawrence College for 38 years. A leading storyteller of his time, he is best known for his magnum opus, "The Hero with A Thousand Faces," a detailed text on the commonalities between the many hero stories of fairy tale, myth, and religion throughout recorded human history. This "monomyth" shows the common trajectory of all great heroes (and ourselves):

The hero leaves home, ventures into the supranatural world, overcomes great obstacles and cultivates new abilities for having done so, and then returns to his ordinary world with more to offer his community.

Every roll is such a journey.

We all have positions and techniques where we have considerably more skill than the rest. These are the "knowns," the ordinary world: pockets of competence in which we experience minimum growth due to our proficiency.

To grow, we must risk failure away from these areas of comfort. We must venture into the "unknown," the supranatural world of trials, tribulations, and subsequent boons to be won.

Every training session presents a choice:

1) The Way of Comfort: pursuing a high probability of momentary success by staying within your field of "knowns," using your competency to achieve positional advancement or submission.

2) The Way of Growth: venturing into the unknown, using unfamiliar techniques, positions, and combinations of each relative to specific training partners, to purposefully place yourself in arenas where you are not strong, so as to acquire strength.

The possibility of failure and opportunity for growth always reside in the same place. As Epictetus said,

> *"If you wish to improve, be content to be thought foolish and stupid."*

But we are hesitant to do so.

Ego, healthy rivalry, the immediate feedback of success, and the desire to succeed in the present moment constantly steer us toward the way of comfort. When comfort calls, we must remember another great lesson from mythology: the gold is always found where the dragons are.

"The cave you fear to enter holds the treasure that you seek."-Joseph Campbell

At the time of this writing, I have one image in my bedroom to remind me of this: a man standing at the edge of a dark cave.

I have always used that anxious feeling in the pit of my stomach to guide my actions. Whenever I am presented with an opportunity, if it scares me, I must do it. This is a pact I have made with myself, and my life has grown in proportion to the extent that I have honored it.

And so has my Jiu Jitsu.

We will grow to the degree that we continually realize our flaws, face them, and overcome them, and this can only be achieved in that unknown world, at the fringes of our current ability. We must make the most of the opportunities within each training session, willfully risking failure so that we may succeed. And we will do this in perpetuity, regardless of belt level.

Mastery Does Not Exist

Let's be clear: you will never master Jiu Jitsu. It is an ideal to strive toward, not a goal to be achieved. The continuum of mastery is as vast as we are finite, and as we have discussed, the more you learn, the more there is to be learned.

And I have found great solace in this truth. Mastery is not a tyrant with which you lord over yourself your inadequacies. Rather, it is a heading for your compass. I recently realized I will not be able to read all the books I want to in my lifetime. After immediate nihilism, a freedom from the self-imposed pressures of conscientiousness washed over me, because to understand the inherent limitations of being brings with it great peace.

To bind oneself to an unattainable goal is to spend one's whole life in a state of feeling incomplete; the goal is the direction, not a destination. It's a cliché, but clichés say far more than their familiarity allows us to hear. When we learn to see mastery as a continuum on which we move, and that there is no end, we can find joy in the daily striving to become more while appreciating what we currently are.

In a realm where failure is constant and paramount, I can think of no better relationship to experience than this.

Summary of Rule #1- Remember That You Are A Work In Progress

We must embrace failure to progress in this art. By venturing into the unknown, we give ourselves the opportunity to develop new abilities. We must do this repeatedly, knowing that there are always new opportunities to fail, regardless of skill level. We will never master this art, but we must daily strive to be better.

You are a work in progress. All good things are.

Rule #2- Narrow Your Immediate Focus

This art is vast, but simply codified: there are only four major positions in Jiu Jitsu. The variations of these and the techniques therein, however, are endless. This world will reveal itself to you in time, but for now, we just need to start your initiation process—because your humanity depends on it.

Live training is when you will learn the most about Jiu Jitsu, and when Jiu Jitsu will have the greatest effect on your personal development. My goal for our white belts, and I believe this should be your goal as well, is simply to learn to do a few things well in each position so that you can effectively take part in live training, the environment which offers the resistance your growth requires.

I believe Jiu Jitsu is an unrivaled vehicle for personal development, but this metaphor implies that you know how to drive.

Your white belt is a learner's permit with which we get behind the wheel and drive for the first time. Do not try to be Jeff Gordon. That comes later.

To be successful from white to blue belt, and to put you in a position to begin learning the intricacies of Jiu Jitsu, your goal should be to acquire a fundamental understanding of what Jiu Jitsu is, and what your goal is in any given moment.

You need only to learn to do a few things well.

The Positional Hierarchy

There are four positions in Jiu Jitsu: guard, side control, mount, and back. These positions lie on a hierarchy of dominance, a continuum of varying control (safety) over one's partner.

Consider them a ladder upon which we ascend:

(Top of the ladder)

You have your partner's back.
You are on top in the mount.
You are on top in side control.
You are on top in the guard.
You are on bottom in the guard.
Your partner has side control.
Your partner has the mount.
Your partner has your back.

(Bottom of the ladder)

Your goal is to continually ascend this ladder, as position by position you increase your control over your partner. With this as the sole focus of their training, students have a clear objective for their actions.

And this offers a good conceptual framework with which to view techniques. Techniques are not ends, they are means. Techniques are the tools with which we ascend the hierarchy of positions. Rather than viewing techniques as entities separate to themselves, learn to see them as the bridges between positions.

Techniques are the tools with which we ascend the positional hierarchy. This may seem overly simplistic or a point of semantics, but I think it is important for the beginning student to deeply engrain this understanding into one's practice.

Too often the beginning student is paralyzed by the seemingly limitless variables in Jiu Jitsu. From my experience, over-communicating this concept to white belts has proved well worth the effort.

And this brings me to our next point.

Forget Submissions While on Bottom (For Now)

Your time spent at white belt is to prepare you for the long journey ahead. As Professor Ricardo Almeida told me the day I earned my blue belt, "A blue belt signifies that you are ready to learn Jiu Jitsu."

Our goal is to get you to that point in the most efficient way.

At white belt, we are building the foundation upon which the rest of your training will occur. The wider the base of this foundation, the higher the potential peak of its summit, and its width is determined by your understanding of the positional hierarchy and your ability to advance within it.

Therefore, I do not encourage our beginning white belts to focus on submissions, for a very specific reason:

Beyond navigating the positions, we first must learn to control our partner's center of mass using ours (either by being hip-to-hip, chest-to-chest, or both). Later, as we progress in our fine motor skills and technical development, we learn to extend that control to individual limbs (the neck included) to elicit a compromising control leading to submission.

Submissions while on top are one thing. Sometimes we find ourselves in dominant positions and it would seem counter-productive to not capitalize. But as a rule, I do not believe beginning students should focus on submitting off their back. Their task is to learn how to defend from off their back and sweep to obtain an advantageous position. This is far more pragmatic and beneficial to the average beginning student.

To clarify: This is my personal philosophy and one I have come to believe as a result of my experiences teaching.

To clarify further: I am not trying to create world champions. My objective is to help the common man or woman cultivate great skill in Jiu Jitsu, and to use the art as a tool for personal development to lead more productive and meaningful lives.

With this aim, I have found that the white belt portion of our journeys (at least the beginning, initiation phase) is best used to get a broad understanding of the hierarchy of positions and the relationships between them. This leads to a better understanding of positional Jiu Jitsu which, in time, produces many opportunities for submission.

The Techniques

Techniques are the tools with which we move along the positional hierarchy. Your goal is to use techniques to ascend this ladder without ever descending.

The bottom portion of the ladder is one of defense, on which we learn to survive compromised positions and advance to safety. Once we reach the middle of the ladder, we are in the realm of the guard. Using the guard on bottom, we learn how to defend ourselves while on our back. It is highly advantageous to learn how to keep someone in your guard, before you begin to learn to advance from this position. Once we can defend, we use sweeps to obtain top position. When we are on top in the guard, our sole focus is to get to a place of more control by passing the guard. And now at the upper end of the ladder, we continually seek to advance position without allowing our partner to do the same.

There are always two people on this ladder. Your ascension means your partner's descent, as your positions are inversely proportional. Every time you ascend a rung, he falls down a rung. The more rungs between you two, the better off you are.

The techniques the white belt should understand are all positional advancements, and can be codified simply as:

- Reversals
    - Being on bottom in side control or mount and using a technique to get on top.
- Guard recoveries
    - Being in a disadvantageous position, regaining control by locking your legs around your partner.
- Sweeps
    - Using your guard to attain top position.
- Guard Passes
    - While on top, freeing yourself from the entanglement of your partner's legs.
- Advancements to more dominant positions
    - Going from side control to mount, and then from mount to back.

In keeping with our ladder metaphor, and understanding that techniques are what you use to ascend the ladder, your goal is simply to have a couple of techniques from each position that will allow you to do so.

Especially in the beginning, you do not need a wide array to do this.

Take the guard for example. There are many guard variations, each with seemingly countless techniques. As you get more experienced, you will explore these deeply. For now, you would do well to learn just a few sweeps and really try to understand them as you utilize them in training. Rather than be paralyzed by choice, find a minimum viable product with which you can consistently advance position.

Because for our purposes, your ability to perform certain kinds of sweeps does not matter. Your ability to sweep matters. And that is a very real and necessary distinction.

So long as you are learning to ascend the ladder, I personally do not care too much with what specific techniques you are doing so. The importance of these comes later.

The white belt should seek to acquire a handful of competent techniques in each position. This will give one the requisite tools necessary to live train effectively, and thus begin to truly learn the subtleties and principles of the art.

Summary Rule #2- Narrow Your Immediate Focus

The positions in Jiu Jitsu follow a hierarchy. Our goal at white belt is to understand this hierarchy, described in this chapter as a ladder, and to learn a few techniques which will help us ascend to positions of more control. Give positions priority in your education over submissions.

You'll have plenty of time for those later.

Rule #3- Learn How To Learn

Our first two rules were big ones, embracing the growth mindset and codifying Jiu Jitsu in an accessible way. Our third rule is at the center of your Jiu Jitsu education, learning how to learn.

Jiu Jitsu is the tool for personal development. The better you get at wielding this tool, the more likely you are to derive benefits from its practice.

My goal for all our students is to help guide them to black belt. Not because I value the expression of technical mastery in this given field, which I do, but because they are more likely to achieve the original goals that brought them into the academy by achieving a black belt. These goals are commonly: self-defense, weight loss, learning a new skill, and being part of a community. All of which are achieved in proportion to the sincere and repeated attendance of the student.

Our primary goals are achieved on the way to black belt.

My humanity has improved to the degree that I have grown as a marital artist. We must be as sincere about our technical development in Jiu Jitsu as we are our personal growth; they are inextricably linked. And to acquire great skill in this art, unless you are a hyper-talented athlete, you must learn how to learn.

Fortunately, the Jiu Jitsu community follows the same structure that has made organized religions and philosophies so accessible.

Take Buddhism, for example: the three foundations of the Buddhist education are the Buddha, the Dharma, and the Sangha; the teacher, the teaching, and the community of disciples. Organized Jiu Jitsu has the same three-pronged approach to education and provides all the necessary external tools for education.

We as a Jiu Jitsu community have done an outstanding job creating these supportive communities.

With these external criteria met, we need to focus on what is internal: the conceptual framework through we interpret our education.

Seeing Techniques For What They Are

In the previous chapter, we described techniques as the bridges with which we ascend the hierarchy of positions. That is what they do; now let's understand what they are.

Techniques are not entities which exist on an island; an arm bar from closed guard is far more than just an arm bar from closed guard. If we are to truly understand this art, we must look more deeply:

Techniques are the manifestations of principles.

For a technique to be effective, it must embody various principles in Jiu Jitsu. These principles are fundamental truths of Jiu Jitsu, specific concepts which yield forecastable results when applied with proper timing.

Early on in our training, we learn the upa reversal from mount. We trap an arm, trap a foot, and upa in the direction of the limbs we have taken away. This is a mount reversal.

At a deeper level of abstraction, however, it is a paramount example of a principle:

Take away a limb, put weight where that limb would have been, forcing your partner, now without a post, to lose top position. Rather than learn this technique in a vacuum, we must understand the principles it embodies so that we can apply this concept to alternative experiences in Jiu Jitsu.

This principle applies anytime someone is on top of us. By understanding how it works, we acquire a precept (and skill) which exists in far more positions than the one which expresses it.

With finite mat time, learning at this level of abstraction will give us the ability to make the most of our training. Techniques are not ends in themselves. They are means by which we ascend the positional hierarchy and the manifestation of the principles which constitute grappling.

When you are a beginning student, your best asset in understanding these principles is your instructor. To make the best use of this opportunity, you must ask him or her questions, ad nauseum.

Ask Questions

The aim of our education is to acquire knowledge which will lead to understanding. There is a big difference between the two; the world is full of knowledge, but genuine understanding is sparse.

Asking questions will be one of the greatest tools for your education, and the simplest codification of what questions to ask is three-fold: What, How, and Why.

The "Whats" are the techniques that we learn each class. The "Hows" are the three or four steps that comprise the technique. The "Whys" are the principles that make the technique worthwhile.

I have found that if you can articulate these three aspects of Jiu Jitsu, you have assimilated your knowledge into understanding. This is the goal of the student, to be able to understand the many aspects of Jiu Jitsu in this tripartite way.

When you begin, all of Jiu Jitsu is unknown, and we often have no conceptual framework with which to codify the various and seemingly unconnected experiences of training. Therefore, we must be purposeful and diligent with our questions.

The students who progress the fastest are those who ask the most questions.

New students often mistake the respectful atmosphere of the academy for one of silence. You are not expected to know everything. And the more sincerely you can communicate your ignorance, in the form of asking questions, the better grip your instructor will have on your understanding and thus will be better equipped to serve you.

No one will teach you what you pretend to know.

Ask as many questions as you can muster. A good instructor will cherish your inquisition. If you get the feeling like you are annoying your instructor, that says more about your instructor than it does you. Ask away. There is no such thing as a stupid question, as each question reveals your understanding (or lack thereof) to your instructor. The more transparent we are about our understanding, the more likely it is to increase.

Ask questions. Whats. Hows. Whys. The further along this progression (toward why) your questions are, the more universally applicable the answers will be.

Keep a Notebook

Now that you are purposefully pursuing knowledge, you need a place to store it.

I best retain my education by keeping a notebook, in which I write down all the techniques (Whats, Hows, and Whys) I learn on a given day, my notable successes and failures, and any questions or hypotheses I have for the next training session.

Throughout all my years of training, I have only met a handful of students who do this. Historically, they are the ones who progress the fastest, barring the freak athletes that progress fastest in everything, regardless of diligence.

We have much going on in our lives outside of grappling, and our memories are fallible. We must be purposeful about our education. I leave the specifics of note-taking to you. The act of note-taking, because it is so worthwhile, is far more important than the way in which you do it (for now).

Imagine if you tried to pass your college courses by passively showing up to class and then taking the final. We had to take notes to codify our education, and revisit it constantly as we absorbed the information. Taking notes in organized education is a universal. Why should your Jiu Jitsu education be any different?

"If you don't have time to do it right, when will you have time to do it again?"- John Wooden

The thing is, you won't have time. We have a finite amount of mat time which determines the degree to which we achieve our potential. We must use this time wisely if we are to glimpse our highest selves.

My choices in life have always been driven by my desire to achieve my potential. Without getting too deep into the metaphysics, I cannot say for certain why I am here, but I know this fleeting life is an absolute miracle, and I operate under the axiom that to do our best with the time we are given has to be a worthwhile use of this gift.

When we opened the Matakas Jiu Jitsu Academy, our first task was to paint the school. In exchange for pizza and conversation, a bunch of my former students and dear friends came together to paint the whole place in a single night. As you now well know, the conversations between Jiu Jitsu practitioners meander, and at some point in the night we all contemplated our greatest fears.

My buddies responded with the usual answers. Snakes. Clowns. I think one of them even said marriage. But mine was different.

My greatest fear is to confront my creator at the pearly gates after a long life. He asks, *Well, Chris, your time on earth has come to an end. How'd you do?* And I confidently say, *You know what, God, I think I did pretty good.*

And then a screen appears in the cloudy heavens, and he begins to show me all the opportunities I was given, all the gifts that came my way, and then shows me all the times I took the easy way out, or acted unkind as I gave way to weakness. He then looks me straight in the eyes and says,

How'd you really do?

This is my greatest fear, and it drives me daily.

We each have a potential within this art. And the closer we get to its achievement, the more likely we are to see equivalent progress in our personal development. Our highest selves and our technical advancement in this art run parallel with one another. We must sincerely seek to master a guard pass as we would our virtues, because at the end of our lives, I have a feeling we will realize they were the same pursuit.

Take five minutes after training to write about your experiences on the mat. Then, in your free time before your next training session, review your notes so you have a better framework with which to most optimally use your next training session.

Ultimately, how we do one thing is how we do all things. The sincerity with which you approach your training will be the same with which you live. Take the time to be a serious student.

Narrow Your Focus in the Immediate

When we ask questions, keep a notebook, and seek to truly understand the fundamentals of Jiu Jitsu, we are purposefully pursuing a real education. And even as a college graduate, I never understood what this meant until I began my journey in Jiu Jitsu.

Quality Jiu Jitsu instruction is structured: led by an articulate and knowledgeable instructor, in a community of peers all seeking the same advancement, a curriculum is followed to ensure a comprehensive and systematized pursuit of education.

The Jiu Jitsu student must have a clear focus for his education. In the beginning, this is largely the responsibility of the instructor, who should give you a clear-cut picture of the direction you're heading and what to seek to understand along the way. But this only gets you so far, as the instructor has too many students to focus adequately on your personal evolution.

We must become a source of our own education.

Along with the aforementioned necessities, you must have a clear and unwavering focus for your training. The more you can narrow your immediate focus, the more likely you are to gain worthwhile knowledge.

My time in Jiu Jitsu can be easily codified by the epochs in which I focused on very specific aspects of training. I have always needed to hyper-attend to one area of grappling, and only once I understood it to the furthest extent I was capable at that time, then I'd move on to new area of study.

You should always have an individual focus aside from that of the weekly curriculum. That way, when you are live training, you have a clearly defined goal based on an honest audit of your current abilities. Choose the one or two techniques, positions, or concepts which keep presenting themselves to you in live training, and focus on them until you truly understand them.

If you are focusing on a specific kind of guard pass, do your best to bring the rolls into that position, and then hyper-focus on that guard pass in your training, taking mental notes of every obstacle you encounter.

There are a finite number of variables to attend to. If you can consistently diagnose them, you will increase your circle of competency until you have a firm grasp of the position and the subtleties therein. Once you learn to view all your training in this systematized way, success is inevitable.

And this success is a product of understanding. Because a purposeful pursuit of education is not a pursuit of knowledge. The world is flooded with knowledge. We need something more.

What we pursue is understanding.

Pursuing Understanding Through Communication

We all learn in different ways. For most of my time in Jiu Jitsu, my main training partner was Max Bohanan, a two-time world champion and an even better human being. Max is gifted in all the ways that I am not. Professor Almeida would show us a technique, and Max would feel it out once or twice, and instantly be proficient.

I, on the other hand, would not be able to use that technique well until I understood why it worked. In the short term, this seemed to slow my progress as a student. In hindsight, this mode of learning forced me to develop the skills to teach well.

The knowledge we possess is of two kinds: articulate knowledge and inarticulate knowledge. Articulate knowledge is embedded in inarticulate knowledge; the things you know, that you don't know you know, greatly outweigh the things you know you know.

A great indicator of your understanding is your ability to communicate why a technique works. Knowledge is what allows you to perform a technique. Understanding is what allows you to teach it. I know what you are thinking: *I am a white belt, aren't we getting ahead of ourselves by evaluating my ability to teach Jiu Jitsu?*

No, we are finally getting to the heart of the matter.

Because the first person you have to teach Jiu Jitsu to is yourself. And we convert knowledge into understanding using the linguistic system with which we communicate to ourselves.

One of the greatest tools for understanding is conversation. Two minds provide the environment for growth, using each other as a sounding board and mutually stress-testing each other's ideas to better formulate their perspective with the help of another.

Ben Franklin attributed much of his success to the Junto Club, a group of high achievers which gathered together to hammer out ideas and better understand themselves, their projects, and their world. As the Zen saying goes, a five-minute conversation with a wise man is worth more than years of solitary study.

We need to be able to have the same kind of conversations with ourselves.

We must become an autodidact, teaching ourselves through inner dialogues in which we present a hypothesis and reflect on our experiences, stress-testing our ideas as we formulate new and better theories having done so.

In the beginning of my practice, when I achieved a guard pass during live training, I would reflect, asking, "Why did that guard pass work?" and then enumerate as many reasons as I was capable, with as clear and concise language as possible.

The longer the list I was able to write, the better I understood the technique. And this is invaluable, because if you do not understand why something works, you are less likely to repeat it in the future.

We are verbal creatures. We think in words. We need to be able to articulate to ourselves an understanding of our successes and failures. When we do this, we come to see that there are more commonalities than differences between the techniques, positions, and concepts of Jiu Jitsu.

In constantly articulating the root of our successes, we better understand the root of success.

Summary of Rule #3- Learn How To Learn

We must be sincere in our learning. Strive to understand the principles behind the techniques, ask as many questions as possible, and keep a notebook to retain your knowledge. Purposefully pursue understanding as you constantly improve your ability to articulate the principles of good grappling.

The more clearly you can do this, the more likely you are to repeat success in the future.

Rule #4- Be Grateful For Your Teammates

I learned this early on, but it was later than it should have been. Our greatest assets in this endeavor are our teammates. Your teammates are just as integral to your development as yourself; we should treat them with equal reverence. Our teammates provide the resistance which fosters our growth. They are the catalyst for our development, and this is so obvious that we often fail to see it.

Jiu Jitsu is problem solving. Each training partner is not an opponent; he is a problem to be solved. The more difficult the problem, the more rewarding the solution will be.

Our teammates each present a unique set of variables which can exist nowhere else: differing sizes, temperaments, games, experience levels, physical attributes, and depths of understanding. Each teammate is a different problem which yields a different treasure. To become a complete grappler, we need to develop the different tools which only a wide array of problems can facilitate.

"The demon you can swallow gives you its power."
-Joseph Campbell

It is these challenges which further our development. Each one of our fellow students is a part of us not yet digested; the bread on the table that becomes our bones. With each presenting a different problem, and each problem yielding different fruits, we want to become a polymath: answering problems across disciplines which yield a greater homogenous understanding of the whole.

Every teammate is a gift, especially those you consider peers or superiors. These present greater challenges which yield exponentially more growth. Their own development holds us to a higher standard.

Beyond the technical necessity that these teammates produce, there is an accompanied social obligation. We are social creatures. We have a biological need to belong to the group. We all seek to rise in our competence hierarchy, garnering more respect from ourselves and the world. If only out of fear of getting left behind, this social pressure will force your evolution with an urgency that you alone could not create.

We cannot do Jiu Jitsu alone. We need each other to practice this beautiful art. We are the sculptor and our partner is our canvas. We need a medium through which we can manifest our greatest creativity and gifts.

We are that medium for each other.

This is why we are all so grateful for each other, high fiving and hugging multiple times after a roll. In our depths, we understand that we were only able to have that experience because of the partner before us. We feel indebted to our partners for giving us the opportunity to feel something so beautiful, intimate, and chaotic.

How Michelangelo felt about his marble when sculpting David, we must feel about each other.

We are forced to venture into our depths in proportion to the skill of our training partner. When I have performed my best Jiu Jitsu, it was only because my partner demanded it, presenting appropriate responses which led to the necessity of something beautiful.

When you share that with someone, it permanently changes your relationship to them, through deep appreciation connecting you in a way which transcends Jiu Jitsu. And for me, these have been the most rewarding aspects of my time in Jiu Jitsu.

The people have always outweighed the art.

What we do is difficult. It is made a lot easier by suffering together with people you love. Those friendships will attract you to the mat more than any solitary motivation. And they will keep you there when you are sore, tired, and sometimes, broken.

The modern world has devalued human relationships to an extraordinary degree. We have metrics for everything except love. Though people are kind, society is not. We are all on guard because most times we must be. Outside of our family and immediate friends, many of us do not experience positive emotions from others.

Jiu Jitsu is different, and we feel it. The academy is an atmosphere of mutual support and fellowship. Part of us wakes that is often forced to stay dormant in our daily lives. We then take this strength and kindness found on the mats and apply it to the real world.

But for many, we find it first on the mats with the exceptional people Jiu Jitsu attracts. I have met some of the most remarkable people through Jiu Jitsu, and that's because the barrier to entry is so high.

When Ernest Shackleton gathered his crew for his now famous Antarctic voyage, he ran an ad in the paper that said:

"Men wanted for hazardous journey, small wages, bitter cold, long months of complete darkness, constant danger, safe return doubtful, honor and recognition in case of success."

After battling the Antarctic conditions for close to two years, with repeated trials of adversity rivaling that of Hercules, all men survived, a living testament to the will of man and the leadership of Shackleton.

If Jiu Jitsu ran an ad, it would read something like this:

Men and women wanted. In an age when we don't have to try for much, where movies are streamed into our homes and pizzas delivered to our doors, come work really hard at something incredibly difficult, where grown men try to choke you. If you like being sore for the rest of your life, always having an injury, getting disfigured and sacrificing countless social occasions to struggle mightily, come play Jiu Jitsu.

Many high caliber men and women answer the ad, and then Jiu Jitsu (like Shackleton) selects only the finest. It is Darwinian. The difficulty of the task self-selects the quality of the individual.

We are surrounded by exceptional people whom we respect and appreciate. As they give us the opportunity to strive toward our highest selves, we do the same for them. It is astonishing that we can be anything but grateful for our teammates.

The way we practice this gratitude is by investing in them, devoting our time to helping them improve their craft, because selfishly, it will help improve ours. Our teammates are extensions of ourselves. They are not just an important part of our development, they are the source of our development. We should treat them as such. As Rudyard Kipling said,

"The strength of the wolf is the pack."

But we forget this. And we forget it across multiple levels of resolution.

We are quick to criticize our society as it infringes upon the freedom of the individual. Yes, culture is a great threat to the individual, but it is also the foundation upon which the individual stands as he reaches for the heavens.

We can only achieve our highest selves within a community.

Jiu Jitsu highlights this truth. To the degree that we can remember this, embody and live it, we will progress through this art in proportion. Too often myopic thinking leads Jiu Jitsu practitioners to act like they are in competition with each other. Egos clash and resentment builds. We learn to see each other as adversaries, even among teammates.

We are each on our own journey, and a big part of that journey is being an aid to the journey of others. Everyone in the academy is simply there to help you become better. And you are there to help everyone else become better. That's it.

It does not matter how our journeys compare to one another. What matters is that we found our own journey and we honor it by acting nobly.

If you have anything but gratitude for the people you train with, you are missing the point. Those subtle animosities and resentments slowly eat us alive. We must let go of these modes of being if we are to grab hold of our highest selves. We are here for each other. We are here to help one another achieve our highest selves through this medium. The rest is nonsense.

Summary of Rule #4- Be Grateful For Your Teammates

Our training partners present unique problems to be solved, which forces our personal evolution. They are the source of our progress, and we cannot do Jiu Jitsu without them. We are not in competition with one another. We are assets for each other as we all pursue our highest selves.

We are on the same team, and not just in Jiu Jitsu.

Rule #5- Jiu Jitsu Is The Vehicle For Something More

We have talked in depth about the various aspects of the Jiu Jitsu experience. There is one final, and most important, aspect to be discussed:

Understanding what Jiu Jitsu is in the context of our lives.

I have always viewed Jiu Jitsu as a tool for personal development, my growth as a person being more important than my ability to pass the guard. It is the best means of self-actualization I have ever found, and continues to be to this day.

 In Stephen King's book *On Writing*, he describes his relationship to writing in the following way:

"It starts with this: put your desk in the corner, and every time you sit down there to write, remind yourself why it isn't in the middle of the room. Life isn't a support-system for art. It's the other way around."

This is my relationship to Jiu Jitsu.

I love Jiu Jitsu and will spend the rest of my life training in this beautiful art. It is the best activity I have ever discovered, but it will always be subordinate to my humanity. It is the vehicle through which we each become more. We are obligated to do this: to make the most of our potential for ourselves, for our neighbor, and out of appreciation for existence itself, no matter the vocabulary you use to describe its source.

We are finite creatures. We only have so many hours within the day to attend to our many responsibilities. We need to use these wisely.

First, we need to define what success is for us, and then allocate our limited hours accordingly to best facilitate its achievement. We have much to attend to: family, health, work, and our individual pursuits, all vying for our finite time. We must offer each of these aspects of our lives, a portion of our lives, to the degree that we value them.

Odds are you are not going to become a world champion. And you probably don't want to. Even if you did, and devoted your life to that aim, you would still spend most of your time in endeavors outside of Jiu Jitsu.

Jiu Jitsu is not a sport to be won. It is an art to be enjoyed and utilized for personal development. It is a conceptual framework through which we interpret experience and mold ourselves. It is the remedy for the stress in our lives, an oil change for the soul. It is the antidote to disease and unhealthiness and disrupts our inclination toward bad habits.

Jiu Jitsu offers the environment which forces our growth. An everchanging problem which, out of necessity, forces our constant adaptation of the mind, body, and spirit. This is the discipline through which we mold ourselves. As the samurai used fighting and calligraphy to train their character, we too must use Jiu Jitsu as the vehicle through which we manifest our potential.

This is possible because Jiu Jitsu reveals ourselves to ourselves. In everything we do, we express what we are. Your "game" in Jiu Jitsu is a mirror which reflects your philosophy. It is transparent to your character, both your strengths and weaknesses. How we respond to adversity on the mat is how we respond in life.

The mistakes we make on the mat, whether from emotion or myopic thinking, are those which we make in our daily lives. They are much easier to see on the mats because your training partners instantly capitalize on your mistake, providing the immediate feedback that life often fails to.

Our bad habits take years to kill us. Their effects come on over time, so we never see them. On the mat, one misstep and we are submitted. We are immediately shown the error of our ways. This allows us to make countless more iterations and accelerate our development.

And that's why training Jiu Jitsu is so important. You receive invaluable reps combating your greatest weaknesses within the safety of the mat. You work through your impatience on the mat rather than while stuck in traffic. The resolve you bring forth amid tired scrambles is the determination with which you face the Sisyphean task of life.

If you develop the proper lens, your game will reveal more of yourself than any psychologist. It will reveal your current disposition while providing countless opportunities to push the boundaries of your depths. Personal development is difficult. If you wish to grow, embody that virtue on the mats first, and it will permeate into the rest of your life.

We all start Jiu Jitsu for different reasons. Some of us to lose weight. Others to learn self-defense. I began because I did not like that there were men of lesser character than myself who could physically hurt me. I suppose you could say I started in fear.

But I continue in love.

Our reasons for staying always differ from the ones that got us started. It is only natural that your relationship to Jiu Jitsu will change as its role in your life does.

Jiu Jitsu has been many things to me. An ego boost. A confidence builder. An identity. A means through which to be conscientious. A community. An escape.

Most importantly, it has always been the vehicle through which I became a better version of myself. That is its greatest reward. And it took receiving a black belt in Jiu Jitsu to learn I am a white belt in everything else. The small degree of competency

I have developed in this art has shown me the complete naivety I possess everywhere else. I have had more opportunities in this art, and probably a more natural propensity toward success, than any other endeavor of my life.

And yet I am still acutely aware that I don't understand Jiu Jitsu to the extent it deserves.

I am a white belt in everything else. And that's okay. But I don't want to be a white belt in my humanity. We owe it to ourselves, our neighbor, and our creator to be better.

We can all use Jiu Jitsu to strive toward our highest selves.

We just need to remember that's the purpose Jiu Jitsu serves. This leaves us tempered in victory and consoled in defeat. There will be many ups and downs throughout our Jiu Jitsu journey.

We must always remember that even more than Jiu Jitsu, we are pursuing ourselves.

Summary of Rule #5- Jiu Jitsu Is The Vehicle For Something More

Jiu Jitsu is the vehicle with which we pursue our highest selves. It is a support system which feeds the rest of our lives, not an obsession to take away from life. It is beautiful, complex, and vast, but cannot hold a candle to our humanity.

Use this art to become a better version of yourself. This is where its greatest value is to be found.

Conclusion

We are a creature that can improve. None of us have glimpsed what we can become, and we can get there, if we keep showing up wisely.

And when we do show up, we must narrow our focus. Jiu Jitsu is too vast and we are too limited to broadly and casually gander, we must be precise in what we seek to understand. The more specific our pursuits, the more clearly we will see this art. We will use this art as a means of learning how to learn, as the purposeful pursuit of understanding evokes a sincerity within us that sees the need for our practice.

In that commitment, we see clearly the value of our training partners. We understand that they are our greatest asset and a part of our journey, that we owe them more than we could ever repay.

But what we owe them most is our own development. We must become a better us, for them.

And that is Jiu Jitsu's greatest reward. It will mold you into the person you always dreamt you could be, that your environment until now has failed to call forth. We must make full use of this opportunity.

These are your five rules for white belt, a conceptual framework with which to better understand your training. It is my sincere hope that they serve you well. The world needs more people fighting on behalf of the Good. And as far as I can tell, there is nothing in Jiu Jitsu but good. Thank you for beginning your practice of this art. I implore you, keep going.

We will all be better as a result.

Notes

Notes

Notes

34958842R00037

Printed in Great Britain
by Amazon